A Walk in the Past

Georgetown

BY

Anthony S. Pitch

MINO PUBLICATIONS
Potomac, Maryland

Published by
Mino Publications, Inc.
9009 Paddock Lane
Potomac, MD 20854

Library of Congress Catalog Card No.
97-73342
ISBN 0-931719-09-7

Printed in the United States of America

For Michael & Nomi

Also by Anthony S. Pitch

The Burning of Washington:
The British Invasion of 1814
(History Book Club selection)
Chained Eagle
(Military Book Club main selection)
Washington, D.C. Sightseers' Guide
Congressional Chronicles
Exclusively White House Trivia
Exclusively Presidential Trivia
Exclusively First Ladies Trivia
Exclusively Washington Trivia
Peace
Bazak Guide to Italy
Bazak Guide to Israel
Inside Zambia - And Out

PREFACE

This walk takes about two hours if you bypass three optional detours. The detours are marked clearly on the center spread map at stop numbers 17, 34, 35, 36, 37, 52, 53, 54 and 55.

If the walk is taken in its entirety it will last about two and a half hours, so long as you do not linger at the many attractive houses in between the pre-selected, numbered stops.

Georgetown is not served directly by the high-speed, electrified Metrorail. The closest Metrorail stop is at *Foggy Bottom* on the Blue and Orange lines, about a 15 minute walk to the commercial heart of Georgetown at the intersection of M Street and Wisconsin Avenue. It is a further 15 minute brisk walk from these crossroads all the way up Wisconsin Avenue to the start of the guided walk at the junction with R Street.

However, Metrobuses go along M Street and up and down Wisconsin Avenue at frequent intervals, stopping just a few feet away from the starting point of this walk.

If you are going by taxi tell the driver to let you off at the Georgetown library, at the intersection of Wisconsin Avenue & R Street NW.

Of course the walk can be done in reverse or even in bits and pieces to suit your own preferences and time limitations. Be advised, though, that doing it in reverse means walking uphill, at a rather slower pace towards the end.

The aging homes are quaint and elegant with graceful lines and distinctive touches.

HISTORICAL HIGHLIGHTS

Georgetown flourished as a sophisticated community long before the founding of Washington, D.C. The first great landowner, an immigrant Scot named Ninian Beall, obtained title early in the 18th century.

The sole remaining survey stone dated 1751 from the Town of George still stands in a private garden near N & 30th Streets. The glorious Old Stone House, at 3051 M Street, was built in 1765 as a carpentry shop with family living quarters above and is believed to be the oldest surviving building in the nation's capital.

Georgetown University was founded in 1789, making it the oldest Catholic institution of higher learning in the country. It chalked up another first in 1873 when Rev. Patrick Healy became the first black president of a major American university. The most famous alumnus is President Bill Clinton from the class of 1968.

A plaque near the Georgetown waterfront at the NW corner of 31st & K Streets marks the site of Suter's Tavern, where in 1791 George Washington negotiated the purchase of land for the city named after him.

When the government moved down from Philadelphia to the village of Washington in 1800, Secretary of the Treasury Oliver Wolcott wrote to his wife that Congressmen looking for comfortable accommodation would have to lodge in Georgetown. Many Congressmen from the South rented rooms in Georgetown, even though it cost them a pretty penny for the daily hackney-coach rides back and forth to the U.S. Capitol.

After Congress declared war on Britain in 1812 the fiercest criticism came from Georgetown, where Alexander Contee Hanson published his anti-war, anti-government newspaper, *Federal Republican & Commercial Gazette* at the corner of 30th & M Streets. When he distributed it in pro-war Baltimore it sparked the worst mob riots the Republic had ever seen.

Two years later British troops routed American defenders at Bladensburg and the ragged militiamen retreated through Georgetown. Dolley Madison fled the President's House (later called The White House), stopping first in Georgetown before crossing into Virginia. That night Georgetowners stared across Rock Creek to the awful spectacle of the British burning the President's House and the Capitol.

The lawyer and poet, Francis Scott Key, had his offices in Georgetown when he composed the words of the Star-Spangled Banner in 1814.

On 4th July 1828 President John Quincy Adams turned the first sod in Georgetown for the Chesapeake and Ohio Canal. It had not turned a profit by the time it reached its western terminus at Cumberland, MD in 1850 because of competition for trade from the faster and more reliable Baltimore and Ohio Railroad.

In 1842 Charles Dickens wrote of his recent visit: *At Georgetown, in the suburbs, there is a Jesuit College, delightfully situated.... The heights of this neighborhood, above the Potomac River, are very picturesque: and are free, I should conceive, from some of the insalubrities of Washington. The air, at that elevation, was quite cool and refreshing, when in the city it was burning hot.*

As the country hurtled towards civil war the depth of passions could be gauged from an incident in 1848 when a ship docked in the Potomac river at the foot of 7th Street and unloaded its cargo of wood. During the night the white crew secretly took on board 77 runaway slaves and set sail downriver. When word reached Georgetown slaveholders the following day they took chase in a steamboat, captured the fugitive schooner at the mouth of the Potomac and hauled it back. The white crew members were saved from lynchings only because they were hustled off to jail.

The Civil War split the town's loyalties. Many of the older, moneyed families, with roots in rural plantations, sided with the South. They were known collectively as The Secesh. At one church feelings ran so strongly against the government that the rector declined to pray for the wellbeing of the President.

Thousands of rowdy and unruly Union troops were billeted in Georgetown's buildings and open fields. They were a constant menace with their brawling, whoring and drunk and disorderly behavior. Union troops vandalized buildings and stole when the opportunity arose. Men from one Massachusetts regiment were taken to task by a newspaper for lounging about in the nude on the banks of the Potomac river, in full view of ladies passing by on river craft and of families traveling by in carriages.

Many of the churches, warehouses and a hotel were converted into Union hospitals. Louisa May Alcott, author of the novel, *Little Women*, was a volunteer nurse for a few weeks in the hospital at the corner of 30th and M Streets, until stricken by typhoid. She was delirious for three weeks during which her yard-and-a-half long hair was cut off and she was fitted with a wig. But she had enough impressions to write a gripping book in 1863 called *Hospital Sketches.*

By the end of the Civil War Georgetown and Washington were sharing the same gas and water systems, the street railway and police. In 1871 Congress fused the two separate city governments into one. That year President Ulysses S. Grant appointed a Georgetowner, Henry Cooke, as the first governor of the combined communities. Later, Georgetown's street names were changed to follow the numerical sequence of those in Washington.

In 1893 the inventor of the telephone, Alexander Graham Bell, was present for ground-breaking ceremonies for the Volta Bureau, corner of 35th St. & Volta Place, which he financed to house the headquarters of the Alexander Graham Bell Association for the Deaf. His workshop was in the carriage house behind his parents' home at 1527 35th St.

Notable Americans buried in Georgetown's Oak Hill Cemetery include President Lincoln's Secretary of War Edwin Stanton, President Truman's Secretary of State Dean Acheson, and the author of *Home, Sweet Home,* John Howard Payne. ❧

Mules still pull canal boats along the C & O Canal in the heart of Georgetown.

Start the walk at the SE corner of R St. & Wisconsin Ave., with your back to the Georgetown library. Look across Wisconsin Ave. to the SW corner.

3308 R STREET

1 This was the final home of Evalyn Walsh McLean, flashy owner of the 44.5 carat Hope Diamond (now in the Smithsonian Institution's National Museum of Natural History on the Mall) who entertained royalty yet died a broken recluse. Her autobiography, *Father Struck It Rich,* should be required reading for anyone still fantasizing about money buying happiness. Here's what happened to Evalyn after she bought the cursed Hope Diamond, when her father's Colorado mine was still bulging with gold. She was in an auto accident with her brother when he was killed. Her son was hit by a car and died. Her daughter died from an overdose of pills. Her husband, Ned, spoiled son of a former owner of the *Washington Post,* died in a Maryland asylum in 1941. She died six years later, having turned away the Chief Justice who came to console her.

After her death this home was carved into a number of residences. Her childhood home, built by father Tom Walsh to upstage rivals among Washington's burgeoning nouveaux riches, still stands at 2020 Massachusetts Avenue, and is now the embassy of Indonesia.

Turn around and walk east along R St. as far as the steps leading up to the library.

SE CORNER R ST. / WISCONSIN AVE.

2 The Georgetown library was built in 1935 on land once known as Lee's Hill when owned by Thomas Sim Lee, Revolutionary War veteran and Governor of Maryland 1779-82 and 1792–94.

Wisconsin Avenue is the route along which American militiamen trudged through Georgetown after being routed by the British at the Battle of Bladensburg in 1814, just before the enemy burned the White House and the Capitol.

Continue along R St. to the home adjacent to the library.

3238 R STREET

3 President Ulysses S. Grant is believed to have rented this red brick Victorian mansion during the last six months of 1865 for $208 a month and after his election as President in 1868 may have used it as the summer White House. Positioned on the highest point of Georgetown, it was much cooler and healthier than the lower malarial swamps of Washington.

First Lady Julia Grant described it as "large but not comfortable," so they moved to a house on I Street in 1866.

President Lincoln visited here during the Civil War when it was the residence of army chief of staff Gen. Henry "Old Brains" Halleck. The sound of buglers at nightly taps and tattoos exasperated some of the neighbors. The house, built in 1857, was bought in 1875 by the poet, Col. John Joyce, who wrote the lines:

Laugh and the world laughs with you.
Weep and you weep alone.

From 1933-35 it was the group home of brilliant young men known as President Roosevelt's Brains Trust, who formulated and drafted much of the New Deal legislation. Among the famous resident legal lions were Tommy "The Cork" Corcoran and Ben Cohen. Recruited by Harvard professor and later Associate Justice of the Supreme Court Felix Frankfurter, they were known as "Frankfurter's hot dogs."

Continue down R St. to the 3rd house on the right.

3210 R STREET

4 Abe Fortas bought this mansion for $250,000 in 1965, the year he was appointed an Associate Justice of the Supreme Court. His cigar-smoking widow, Carolyn Agger, who headed the tax division of the top-notch legal firm of Arnold and Porter, died in 1996.

Fortas was nominated by his close friend, Lyndon Johnson, to be chief justice in 1968 but the nomination was withdrawn after Senate opposition to his having assisted and advised the President while he sat on the high court bench. Fortas resigned from the Supreme Court in 1969 amid a scandal involving a securities swindler.

Justice Fortas was an accomplished violinist whose Sunday evening house concerts featured his famous virtuosi friends, Isaac Stern, Rudolf Serkin, David Oistrakh and Pablo Casals.

Continue down R St. to 32nd St. Look diagonally across the road at the public entrance to the large estate.

1703 32ND STREET

5 Dumbarton Oaks, now open to the public, was built about 1800 then added to and rebuilt several times by different owners. It was called Dumbarton by the first owner of the land, an immigrant Scotsman, after a Scottish landmark. A much later owner called it The Oaks. The famous South Carolinian politician, John C. Calhoun, lived here when he was a U.S. Senator and Vice President under John Quincy Adams. In 1920 the run-down place was bought and restored by Robert and Mildred Bliss, a married couple who are buried in the landscaped grounds. He had been ambassador to Sweden and the Argentine.

Top officials of the U.S. Britain, the Soviet Union and China met at Dumbarton Oaks during World War 11 to define a new organization which would be known as the United Nations.

Composer Igor Stravinsky's Concerto in E Flat is known as the Dumbarton Oaks Concerto because it was commissioned by the Bliss's and first performed here.

The Bliss's donated the 16-acre estate and their vast collection of pre-Columbian and Byzantine art and artifacts to Harvard University.

There is much to admire in 10 acres of gardens, which include seasonal plantings.

Continue down R St., turn right at 31st St. & go to the 5th house on the right.

1688 31ST STREET

6 Known nationally as "Mr. Republican" because of his great influence in the GOP, Senator Robert Taft and his wife, Martha, lived here from 1941 until his death in 1953.

Everyone knew that Taft, Senate Republican leader and son of President William Howard Taft, had terminal cancer. Imagine the surprise of a Capitol Hill aide who came to this house on legislative business in 1953 and saw the ailing senator paging through a Sears & Roebuck catalogue. The stricken man then wrote out an order for a new refrigerator, even though he knew his days were numbered. The aide was filled with admiration. The doomed man died just a few weeks later.

His political legacy survives because he co-authored the Taft-Hartley Act of 1947 which curbed the activities and powers of trade unions. A statue of Taft stands close to the U.S. Capitol.

Continue down past 2 houses. Look across the road.

1669 31ST STREET

7 This was the home of Francis Biddle, who was attorney general in World War 11 when he prosecuted eight German spies and saboteurs who had landed on the coasts of Florida and Long Island in 1942. Six of them were executed that year in Washington.

After the war Biddle was the American chief judge at the international war crimes trials in Nuremberg, where 10 top Nazis were hanged. After the trials Biddle reported to President Truman that the judgment showed "aggressive war is criminal and will be so treated."

Biddle was chairman of Americans for Democratic Action in the 1950s when he spoke out against two Republicans, his neighbor, Sen. Robert Taft, and the infamous Sen. Joe McCarthy, for what he called "an amazing contempt for civil liberties."

Biddle's wife, Katherine Garrison Chapin, was a poet, playwright and fellow of the Library of Congress. They were close friends of the Welsh poet Dylan Thomas, who was their house guest. When the poet made off with two of Biddle's shirts after one visit, the host quipped, "I hope they fit."

In 1957 the Biddle's valuable collection of paintings by Picasso, Toulouse-Lautrec, Matisse, Degas and Vlamnick was exhibited at the Corcoran Gallery.

Biddle's family had been in public life from the earliest days of the Republic. His maternal great-great-grandfather, Edmund Randolph, was the first attorney general.

In 1814 William Thornton stood here and watched the British burn the Capitol he had designed.

Continue down 31st St. as far as the ornate gate on your right.

1644 31ST STREET

8 Surely the most poignant moment of the War of 1812 took place on the night of Wednesday, August 24, 1814 when Dr. William Thornton stood in this hilltop mansion and watched the British burn the magnificent U. S. Capitol he had designed. Thornton and his wife Anna Maria fled here from their Washington home earlier that day when they saw routed American militiamen escaping to Georgetown and beyond after the battle of Bladensburg.

Thornton designed this neoclassical mansion for Martha Washington's granddaughter, Martha Custis Peter and her husband, Thomas. It was completed in 1816. Mrs. Peter was such an anglophile that she called the estate Tudor Place and named one of her daughters Britannia.

The ancestral mansion was handed down to successive generations of the Peter family until

1988 when it was opened to the public. It is exquisitely furnished with period pieces and other memorabilia from the earliest residents.

Continue down 31st St., cross Q St., turn right along Q to the 4th house on the left.

3112 Q STREET

9 Katherine Anne Porter geared up for the last part of her international bestselling novel, *Ship of Fools,* in this house in 1961. After it was published on April Fool's Day the following year, the film rights sold for $400,000 and the movie starred Vivien Leigh, Simone Signoret, Jose Ferrer and Lee Marvin.

It made her rich and internationally famous. But she could not shake off her childhood demons. She was forever ashamed of having been born into a poor and what she called an undistinguished family. So she fantasized. She was born Callie Porter and invented the name Katherine Anne. She told people she came from an old Southern family with plenty of servants. She even copied out the crest of an ancient Porter family from the Congressional Record and claimed it as her family's. And if she learned of a distinguished Porter from the past, she claimed him as an ancestor. When she went out she often dressed in hat and gloves, telling people she had been brought up that way. In reality, she was raised dirt poor on a Texas farm.

In 1977, a Maryland court authorized a guardian to protect her considerable assets. She was partially paralyzed, confined to her bed, and at times unintelligible. The stylish novelist and evocative short story writer, who won a Pulitzer Prize and the National Book Award, died in a Silver Spring, Md. nursing home in 1980 at the age of 90.

Return to the corner, go right into 31st St. to the 3rd house on the right.

1528 31ST STREET

10 After his election to the House of Representatives in 1946 John F. Kennedy rented this row house for three years, paying $300 a month when he moved in at the beginning of 1947. He shared it with his sister, Eunice, who was then an executive secretary in the Justice Department. His family sent along the cook who had been with them since he was a small boy.

While living here in 1948 he learned that his sister, Kathleen, a former journalist on the Washington *Times-Herald,* had been killed in a plane crash in France.

Return to the corner, turn right into Q St., passing the church on your right.

3028 Q STREET

11 Sinclair "Red" Lewis lived here in 1926, four years before he became the first American to win the Nobel Prize for Literature. He was something of a scoundrel - a tall, red-haired nomad who was often drunk and outspokenly atheistic. When the Daughters of the American Revolution twice banned him from Constitution Hall he claimed it as an honor.

In 1925 he refused the award of a Pulitzer Prize for his book *Arrowsmith,* which, like all his novels, poked fun at small town life and provincialism. Lewis objected to Pulitzer's will which said award-winning books had to "represent the wholesome atmosphere of American life."

In 1926 he and his then wife, Grace, rented this house for $600 a month, with three servants totaling another $200 p.m. In November he went to New York and returned for the Christmas festivities. When he got drunk at a dinner party his wife upbraided him in public. He stared at her, walked out, left for New York and never returned.

Meanwhile his publisher was preparing to print 140,000 copies of his new novel, *Elmer Gantry,* then the largest first print run for a hardback book.

After its publication he appeared at a church in Kansas City, Missouri, put his watch down on the pulpit, and said if God was vengeful as portrayed by Fundamentalists He would strike Lewis dead within 15 minutes. After a quarter of an hour he picked up his watch and left. The unconventional author, who was born in a tiny Minnesota town, died 24 years later in Rome.

Look directly across the road to the house soaring above the others.

3027 Q STREET

12 This is where you get to live when you're the nation's most celebrated investigative reporter. Bob Woodward has lived here since earning fame and fortune for his role in uncovering the Watergate scandal.

He was a 29-year-old lowly reporter on the Metro desk of the *Washington Post* when burglars were arrested at the Democratic National Committee headquarters in the Watergate on June 17, 1972.

Woodward and his colleague Carl Bernstein wouldn't let go of the story until they got to the bottom of it. The result was Richard Nixon's downfall, a Pulitzer for the *Post* and legendary status for Woodward and Bernstein.

When a movie was made of their book, *All The President's Men,* Robert Redford played Woodward and Dustin Hoffman starred as Bernstein.

Woodward's bestselling books proved his uncanny access to the most secret institutions.

Walk down Q St., stopping opposite the 2nd house away from the one you have just seen.

3021 Q STREET

13 After graduating from the University of Virginia Medical School he won international fame as the army doctor who helped stamp out yellow fever. His name was Dr. Walter Reed and he lived in this house during the 1890s.

In 1900 he headed a study of an epidemic of yellow fever in Cuba, which had killed more American troops than bullets during the Spanish-American War. Walter Reed proved the disease was transmitted by mosquitoes. When the insect bit an infected person or animal the yellow fever virus developed inside the mosquito. As soon as it bit another person or animal, the mosquito would pass on the disease. His earlier experiments showed that flies and dust helped spread typhoid.

He was only 52 when he died after an appendectomy in 1902 but he had become so famous that the Walter Reed Army Medical Center in Washington was named in his honor. The stone above his grave in Arlington National Cemetery is etched with the words: *He gave to man control over that dreadful scourge - Yellow Fever.*

Henry Cooke, a banker and friend of President Ulysses S. Grant, built this row of four double houses shortly after the Civil War. Known as Cooke's Row, the two on either end are in the French Second Empire style with Mansard roofs while the two in the center are Italianate Gothic.

Continue down Q St. and cross 30th St.

1537 30TH STREET, SE CORNER

14 Francis Dodge, son of a shipping magnate of the same name, built this sumptuous mansion in 1853 in the style of a 17th century

The home of Henry Cooke, first territorial governor of the District of Columbia.

Italian villa. It was designed by Andrew Jackson Downing, famous for landscaping parts of the Capitol, White House, Mall and Lafayette Square, and his partner, English immigrant Calvert Vaux. When the Dodge family business went bankrupt a few years later, Francis had to sell and moved out.

The banker, Henry Cooke, bought it and added a wing in the south. In 1871 President Ulysses S. Grant appointed him the first territorial Governor of the District of Columbia. Cooke continued to live here and entertained extravagantly during his two years in office, once hosting the President and

1000 guests on Washington's birthday.

Henry moved out after declaring bankruptcy a few years later, though he later recouped much of his losses in mining and railroads.

Two large wings were added to the east and south in 1903 and it is now a sprawling complex of apartments, with many original moldings, doors and fireplaces.

Continue along Q St. and cross 29th St. Look across to the NE corner.

2823 Q STREET

15 A top State Department official who lived here was reportedly threatened by then Attorney General Bobby Kennedy. Under Secretary of State Chester Bowles had apparently gone around saying he didn't agree with the Kennedy administration policies during the early days of the Cuban missile crisis. Word got out that Bobby Kennedy took him by the coat collar and hissed, "You're with us all the way in this, right."

Continue down Q St., cross 28th St. & turn around.

1534 28TH STREET, SW CORNER

16 Robert Dodge, son of a Georgetown shipping magnate, built this mansion in 1853 as a mirror image of the house raised by his brother Francis a few hundred yards further back along Q Street. Unlike his brother, Robert survived the collapse of the family shipping business because he was no longer involved, being owner of a flour mill. Robert Dodge lived in this house until his death in 1887.

The new look dates from 1938-1954 when it was owned by Edith Eustis, granddaughter of the banker William Wilson Corcoran and daughter of Levy Morton, Governor of New York and Vice President under Benjamin Harrison. She added a library and other rooms above a new garage and enclosed part of the veranda.

The palatial mansion was bought for a reported $4 million in 1988 by Boyden Gray, White House counsel during the Bush administration.

For an optional detour cross Q St. & walk uphill on 28th St. for a few hundred yards to the end of the brick wall and entrance gate to private property on the right.

If you do not take the detour walk further down Q St. to the 3rd house from the NE corner, on the left, picking up the narrative at stop #18.

1623 28TH STREET

17 Parts of this estate called *Evermay* were built in the last decade of the 18th century by Samuel Davidson, a Scottish immigrant who made a fortune in real estate, including what is now Lafayette Square facing the White House.

Davidson was a fearsome tycoon who warned trespassers "to avoid *Evermay* as they would a den of devils or rattlesnakes." When he died his will stipulated that the residue of his estate be given to a nephew, Lewis Grant, on condition he immigrate from Scotland and add the name Davidson "as soon as possible" and "forever thereafter." Grant was quick to comply and lived out his life on this estate.

The 3.5 acre property was bought in 1923 by Lamot Belin, an architect and diplomat, who restored the mansion, developed the grounds and passed it on to his descendants. The magnificently landscaped gardens, inspired by travels abroad, have terraces with ornamental pools, statuary, fountains, and a Chinese pavilion beside the tennis court.

Return to Q St., turn left and walk to the third house on the left.

2723 Q STREET

18 Allen Dulles, Director of the Central Intelligence Agency under Presidents Eisenhower and Kennedy, lived here for years until his death in 1969.

On two momentous occasions the telephone rang in this stately home during his retirement. Both times President Johnson was on the line. A week after Kennedy's assassination, the new president called to say he was appointing Dulles to the Warren Commission to investigate the killing. In 1964, after two white and one black civil rights activists disappeared in Mississippi, President Johnson phoned again to order Dulles down south for delicate meetings with the governor and community leaders.

A plaque in the entrance lobby of CIA headquarters in Langley, Virginia, built during his tenure, honors Dulles with the words, *His monument is around us.*

Continue down to the next building on the same side of the road.

2715 Q STREET

19 Washington was a city of fear and pandemonium on Wednesday, August 24th, 1814. The country was at war with Britain and that afternoon enemy troops had rolled over American forces six miles east of the capital at Bladensburg. Most of the residents had fled to the woods and surrounding countryside. President Madison had gone to the battlefield leaving First Lady Dolley Madison at the The President's House (now called the White House). She refused to escape until the Gilbert Stuart portrait of

Dolley Madison fled from the White House to this mansion as the British advanced on Washington.

George Washington was taken down from the wall and removed to safety on a distant farm.

Then she climbed into her waiting carriage to join the last of the refugees and fled to Georgetown. First she stopped at the home of Navy Secretary William Jones. For almost two centuries rumor had it that she later stayed in this mansion, then called *Bellevue* and owned by Charles Carroll, and now called Dumbarton House.

The National Society of the Colonial Dames of America, headquartered here, could never find evidence of Dolley Madison's visit. In 1996, while writing a book on the burning of Washington in 1814, I was researching the personal files of the Navy Secretary, tucked away in Philadelphia, when I found the documentary proof of Dolley Madison's brief refuge in this mansion.

A handwritten memorandum by Navy Secretary William Jones recalls details of the day British troops occupied and burned the White House, the Capitol, the Treasury and other public buildings in 1814:

"I left the Navy Yard at about half past three o'clock accompanied by Mr. Duval and not long after learned that our army was rapidly retreating and that of the enemy advancing rapidly. We proceeded to Georgetown where I met my family and that of the President at the house of Charles Carroll Esq. of Bellevue and received a message from the President requesting that I would join him at Foxall's works. At about 5 o'clock I set out in company with the family of the President, of Mr. Carroll's and my own, with Mr. Duval, and proceeded through Georgetown to join the President....."

Dumbarton House, now maintained as a house museum with period furniture, is open to the public.

Go back along Q St., turn left into 28th St., and right into P St. to the 2nd house on the right.

2805 P STREET

20 Harry Truman's debonair Secretary of State, Dean Acheson, bought this house in 1922 without having seen the inside. He and his wife, Alice, fell for it at first glance but didn't want to disturb the occupants so they wrote asking if they intended buying it. The couple said they were about to move out so the Achesons bought it and only stepped inside after the others left.

Acheson gave a farewell lunch party here on Harry Truman's last day in office. Hundreds of cheering fans thronged the street. Truman later wrote to Acheson that he had never been to such a party "where everybody seemed to be having the best time they ever had."

The Achesons planned on moving to a larger house in the 1930s but their three children objected, saying all their friends were in the neighborhood, so the parents stayed and enlarged the house with three floors in the front and back and two floors in the middle, connected by arched windows.

Acheson is buried beside the Renwick Chapel in Oak Hill Cemetery. His widow, who sold this house in the 1980s, was an accomplished painter whose works were exhibited at the Corcoran Gallery and Phillips Collection. She lived to be 100 years old and died in 1996.

Turn around and look directly across the road.

2808 P STREET

21 The Camelot Couple rented this house for less than a year in 1957 when John F. Kennedy was a U.S. Senator. They moved to Georgetown after selling their Hickory Hill estate in McLean, Virginia to his brother, Bobby. The future president disliked the congested commute from Virginia to Washington, and the McLean home had unhappy associations because of Jackie's miscarriage while resident there.

Move up to the next house on the right hand side.

2811 P STREET

22 These unique and attractive gun-barrel fences were put up by locksmith Reuben Daw in the middle of the last century. He got

hold of muskets from the Mexican-American War of 1848, rammed the stock ends into the ground and spiked the muzzles. Daw lived in this house, as did community activist John Ihlder 70 years later.

Ihlder and other preservationists met here in the 1920s and 1930s to protest unsuccessfully against the first traffic light at Wisconsin and M, the removal of cobble stones from P St., and bus service to Q St. But they did succeed in getting zoning laws outlawing new apartments and hotels in Georgetown's residential areas.

Continue along P St., cross 29th St. to the 2nd house on the right.

2905 P STREET

23 Alger Hiss, believed to have been an American traitor and a Cold War spy, lived in this house in 1935 and 1936. He spent almost four years in prison for perjury in denying that he passed classified State Department documents to a self-confessed Communist. Hiss could not be charged with espionage because a three-year statute of limitations had expired.

Young Congressman Richard Nixon became a household name after taking the lead in accusing Hiss of being a Communist spy. Hiss denied the charges to his dying day in 1996.

The scandal broke when Whittaker Chambers, a former *Time* magazine editor, said Hiss had supplied him with secret State Department documents in the 1930s. Chambers led investigators from the House Un-American Activities Committee to his Maryland farm one December night in 1948 and extracted five rolls of microfilm from a hollowed-out pumpkin.

Chambers admitted he had been a Communist for 14 years and that he had lied to a Grand Jury to protect other Communists, but said he was exposing Hiss to atone for his own past Communist ties. He said he had renounced Communism as evil in 1938.

The trial for perjury caused a sensation because Hiss had clerked for Supreme Court Justice Oliver Wendell Holmes, been secretary general of the organizing conference of the United Nations, advised President Roosevelt and held office as president of the Carnegie Endowment for International Peace. Justice Felix Frankfurter, who taught Hiss at Harvard, was a character witness. Secretary of State Dean Acheson refused to turn his back on Hiss, a long-time friend, even after conviction.

The case continues to be controversial. In 1992, the Russian general in charge of Soviet military intelligence archives, said Hiss had never been recruited as an agent.

Continue along P St., cross 30th St. to the house on your right with granite steps and distinctive wrought iron railing.

3019 P STREET

24 This elegant house was built in 1830 by Edward Magruder Linthicum, a rich hardware merchant, civic leader and philanthropist who bequeathed $50,000 for a school for the free education of white boys in Georgetown.

There was no electricity in the house during the more than eight decades that Miss Mary Zeller lived here until her death in 1934. She made do with gas jets, candles and oil lamps. Zeller once remarked that "it does not seem to matter where you live as long as it is in Georgetown." She had furniture handed down by her great uncle, Dr. William Beanes, who was captured by British troops after they burned Washington in 1814 and

Built in 1830, this elegant home did not have electricity until a long-time resident died in 1934.

detained with Francis Scott Key during the bombardment of Fort McHenry, when Key composed the words of the Star-Spangled Banner.

Continue on P St. for a few paces and look across the road.

3026 P STREET

25 Secretary of State Henry Kissinger moved to this rental home in the waning months of the Gerald Ford presidency and stayed on after linking up with Georgetown University's Center for Strategic & International Studies and teaching diplomacy at the univer-

sity's School of Foreign Service.

The Kissingers are believed to have rented for less than the asking rental of $2500 monthly because of the security improvements, including installation of bullet-proof glass panels over the front windows and new door and window locks requiring 70 keys, mostly for use by the security agents, who also had to outfit their command center room inside.

Continue along P St., crossing Dumbarton Rock Ct. to the NE corner of 31st St.

3053 P STREET

26 Kennedy clan patriarch, Joe Kennedy and his wife Rose rented this Victorian home during the inaugural festivities for their son, John F. Kennedy.

Built in 1876 by the wealthy lumber merchant John Libbey, it used to look like the typical Victorian town home with a front porch, pillars and a bay window. The new look dates from 1928. A scene was shot here for the 1984 movie, *St. Elmo's Fire.*

The house was scooped up for $2 million in 1989 by a partner in a Washington law firm. A contemporary advertisement said there were nine bedrooms, a music room and paneled library.

Cross 31st St. & continue on P St., looking to the 5th house up on the left.

3108 P STREET

27 One of the most famous generals in the Union Army lived here after the Civil War. Gen. George Thomas was also known as *The Rock of Chickamauga* - named for the Tennessee lake where his 25,000 men successfully resisted 65,000 Confederates.

Georgetown

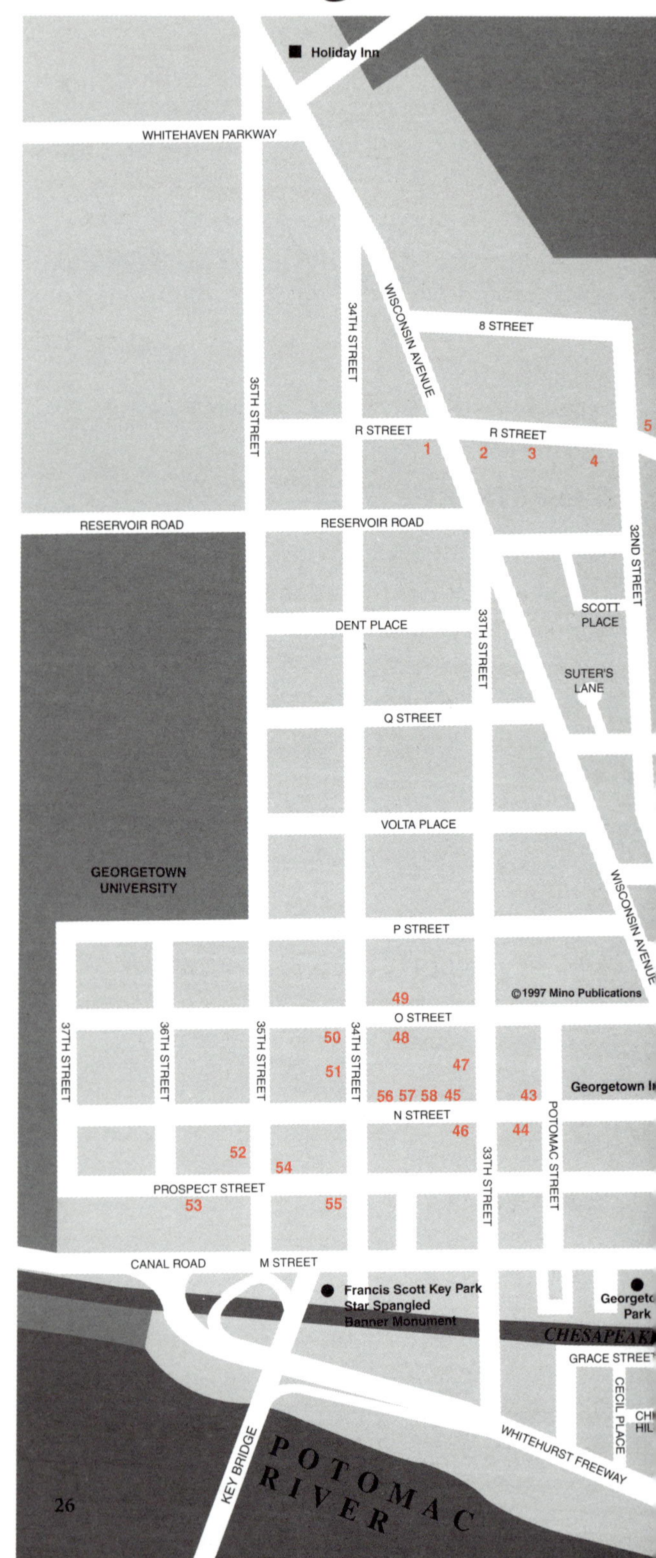

Holiday Inn
WHITEHAVEN PARKWAY
35TH STREET
34TH STREET
WISCONSIN AVENUE
8 STREET
R STREET
R STREET
1
2
3
4
5
RESERVOIR ROAD
RESERVOIR ROAD
32ND STREET
DENT PLACE
33TH STREET
SCOTT PLACE
SUTER'S LANE
Q STREET
VOLTA PLACE
GEORGETOWN UNIVERSITY
WISCONSIN AVENUE
P STREET
©1997 Mino Publications
49
O STREET
37TH STREET
36TH STREET
35TH STREET
50
34TH STREET
48
47
51
56 57 58 45
43
Georgetown I
N STREET
46
44
POTOMAC STREET
52
54
33TH STREET
PROSPECT STREET
53
55
CANAL ROAD
M STREET
Francis Scott Key Park
Star Spangled
Banner Monument
Georget
Park
CHESAPEAK
GRACE STREE
CECIL PLACE
KEY BRIDGE
POTOMAC
RIVER
WHITEHURST FREEWAY

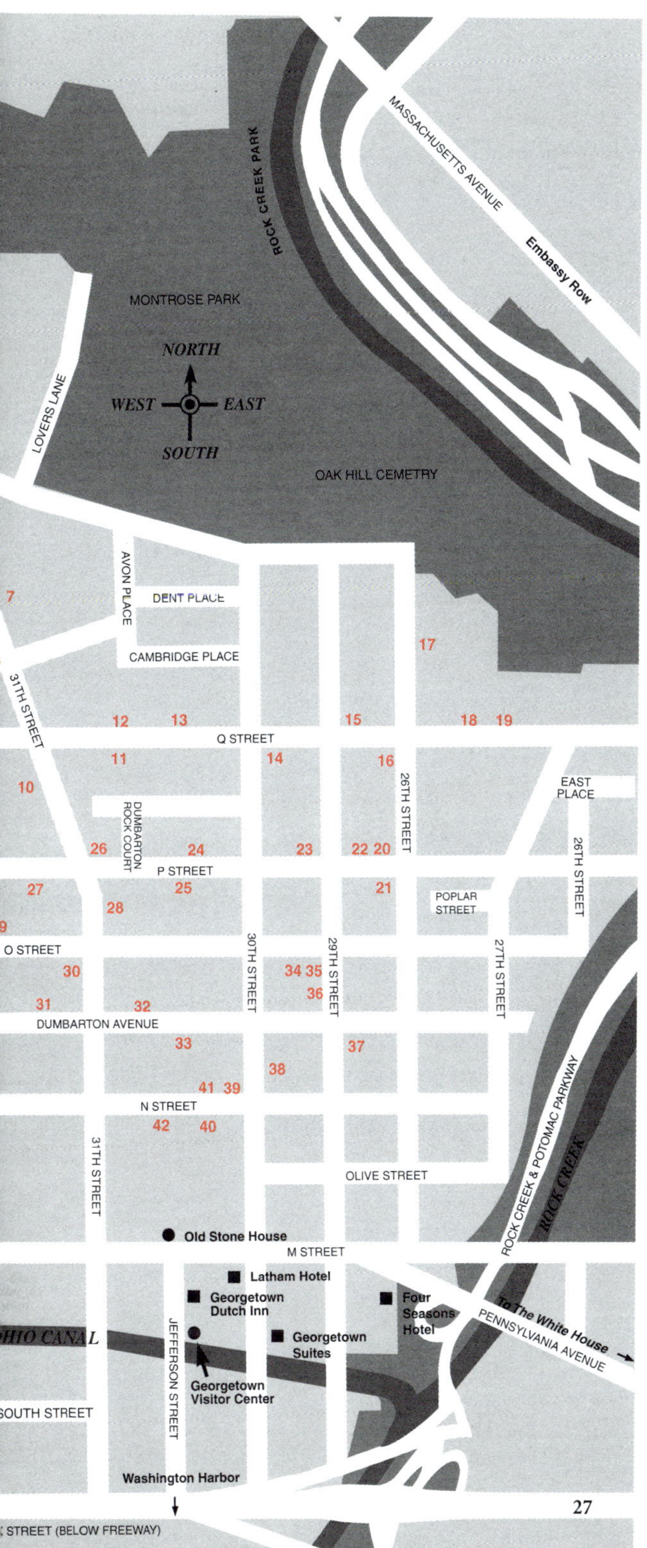
MASSACHUSETTS AVENUE
Embassy Row
ROCK CREEK PARK
MONTROSE PARK
NORTH
WEST
EAST
SOUTH
LOVERS LANE
OAK HILL CEMETRY
AVON PLACE
DENT PLACE
CAMBRIDGE PLACE
31TH STREET
Q STREET
26TH STREET
EAST PLACE
DUMBARTON ROCK COURT
P STREET
POPLAR STREET
O STREET
30TH STREET
29TH STREET
27TH STREET
DUMBARTON AVENUE
N STREET
OLIVE STREET
ROCK CREEK & POTOMAC PARKWAY
ROCK CREEK
Old Stone House
M STREET
Latham Hotel
Georgetown Dutch Inn
Four Seasons Hotel
Georgetown Suites
Georgetown Visitor Center
To The White House
PENNSYLVANIA AVENUE
JEFFERSON STREET
SOUTH STREET
Washington Harbor
STREET (BELOW FREEWAY)
7
9
10
11
12
13
14
15
16
17
18
19
20
21
22
23
24
25
26
27
28
30
31
32
33
34
35
36
37
38
39
40
41
42

In 1879 President Rutherford Hayes and 50,000 people attended the unveiling of his bronze equestrian statue at Thomas Circle, on Massachusetts Avenue and 14th Street, after a huge military parade through the streets of Washington.

During World War 11 the house was bought by freshman Congressman Christian Herter. After his election as Governor of Massachusetts he rented the house to CIA Director Allen Dulles. In 1952, while director-designate Dulles was living here, his sister, Eleanor, had a nightmare in her McLean, Virginia home. She dreamed that Allen Dulles's son, a Marine lieutenant, was crying out for help. She raced over to this house and let herself in with her own key before 7 am. Her brother told her he had just received word from the Korean War front that his son had been wounded in combat. The young man had brain injuries from shrapnel and never recovered fully.

Herter continued to live here after his appointment as Secretary of State in 1959. When the Soviet leader Nikita Krushchev visited Washington, Mrs. Herter hosted a dinner here for Mrs. Nina Krushchev and the American guests sang *For She's A Jolly Good Fellow.*

Mrs. Herter christened the aircraft carrier *Constellation,* from whose decks American planes carried out the first bombing raids over North Vietnam in 1964 - detailed in *Chained Eagle,* my biography of the longest-held American POW in North Vietnam.

Backtrack, go right into 31st St. to the 5th house on the left.

1407 31ST STREET

28 A disgraced U.S. senator lived here in his final two years in that exclusive club. Sen. Thomas Dodd, a Connecticut Democrat, was

censured by the U.S. Senate in 1967 for using campaign contributions for his personal benefit. When the Democrats denied him nomination for a third term, Dodd ran as an independent and finished third. Dodd died less than a year later.

Continue down 31st., turn right into O St. to the flight of wooden steps on the right.

3131 O STREET

29 On March 27, 1935 the Secretary of War pinned a Medal of Honor on the coat of 91-year-old Gen. Adolphus Greely in this house while a military band played the national anthem on the street outside. The rare honor came half a century after Greely's bravery as leader of marooned and starving Americans in the frozen arctic. The scientific expedition of 25 Americans had set out set from Newfoundland in 1881 as part of an international effort to collect data on the Arctic region.

Greely's team got to within 400 miles of the North Pole, penetrating further north than anyone previously. But they missed their rendezvous with a relief ship when it was crushed by icebergs. Two other relief ships failed to get through. When their rations ran out the Americans ate plants, insects, seal thongs, small fish and even their shoes, clothing and sleeping bags. To keep their spirits up Greely held daily prayers and lectured on American history and geography.

Three years after they left Newfoundland a relief ship finally broke through. There were only seven survivors. Seventeen had died of cold and starvation. One man had been shot dead on Greely's orders for stealing food rations.

The Medal of Honor was awarded by special act of Congress because the statute of limitations had expired and the bravery was for an act unre-

The Medal of Honor was pinned to the coat of a 91-year-old general in this brick home.

lated to combat with an enemy. Greely, who became the Army's chief signal officer, died a few months after the award.

Go back to 31st St. and cross O St.

31ST/O STREETS, SW CORNER

30 Among the founders of Christ Episcopal Church in 1817 were many conservative, old-moneyed Maryland landowners and the Georgetown lawyer and poet Francis Scott Key. This third and current building on the corner stand dates from 1885.

Church archives record the 1842 marriage of Britannia Peter, great-granddaughter of Martha Washington, and Commodore Beverly Kennon. Just two years later he was killed, together with the Secretary of State and Secretary of the Navy, when a new gun exploded during test firing aboard a frigate on the Potomac river.

Sentiment was so much in favor of the Confederacy during the Civil War that the Rev. Dr. William Norwood, a southerner himself, abandoned his post rather than obey the Bishop of Maryland, who ordered prayers for a Union victory and the wellbeing of the president.

Go down 31st St. & turn right to the 2nd house on the right.

3107 DUMBARTON AVENUE

31 Dulles International Airport is named in honor of Secretary of State John Foster Dulles, who lived here briefly in 1951 before moving out of Georgetown. The honor was conferrred after his death by President Eisenhower, who attended the formal dedication of the airport by John F. Kennedy in 1962. Republican John Foster Dulles traveled so much by plane that people said he took to the air to avoid being a sitting duck for Congressional Democrats.

This was also the rented home of Bert Lance, briefly Jimmy Carter's first Director of the Office of Management and Budget until forced to resign over questionable past banking practices. His wife, LaBelle, said they "yelled and fussed and cried and prayed" before he quit, denying any wrongdoing. Lance once opined that "sleep's a habit" and that he could get by on less that his usual four hours a night if he had to.

Harold Ickes lived here as White House Deputy Chief of Staff during President Clinton's first term.

Go back to 31st St., cross to the other side of Dumbarton Ave.,cross 31st. St. walk about 40 paces & look across the road.

3037 & 3035 DUMBARTON AVENUE

32 The two coupled houses high above street level have belonged for years to an unlikely pair of celebrity neighbors. Above the right hand steps is the home of J. Carter Brown, the urbane and distinguished former director of the National Gallery of Art. Perched in her aerie atop the left hand steps is the literary vulture, Kitty Kelley, a bestselling, unauthorized biographer who tore the flesh off Nancy Reagan, Elizabeth Taylor and Frank Sinatra before picking clean the remains of the British royal family.

The early 19th century homes were a single family unit for about 100 years before being split in two.

Continue down the right side of Dumbarton Ave.

3018 DUMBARTON AVENUE

33 Supreme Court Associate Justice Felix Frankfurter paid $34,000 for this house in 1947. Twenty seven years later Secretary of State Henry Kissinger rented it during Gerald Ford's presidency. When Kissinger moved out it was taken over by his successor, Secretary of State Cyrus Vance. The townhouse backs up against the N St. mansion bought by Jackie Kennedy soon after President Kennedy's assassination.

In 1975 a tabloid reporter tried to make off with Kissinger's plastic trash bags until his security agents sprang into action. However, they had to free the scribe and garbage when it was learned he had done nothing illegal. The trash contained the names and work and travel schedules of the security agents assigned to protect

Built in 1810, this medieval-style English brick cottage holds African-American church archives.

Kissinger, then code-named *Woodcutter.*

The Kissingers were told to move out while he was still Secretary of State in 1976 when the landlady said the lease had gone on for too long.

For another optional detour continue down Dumbarton Ave., turn left up 30th St. & right into O St. to the small house set back behind the picket fence on the right.

If you do not take the detour turn right at 30th St., picking up the narrative at stop #38.

2906 O STREET

34 This quaint building dates from 1810 and is believed to be the only remaining medieval-style English brick cottage in the District of Columbia. It was restored in 1985 and has a long association with the African-American community in Georgetown.

Known as Heritage House, it contains the archives of adjacent Mt. Zion United Methodist Church - the oldest African-American congregation in Washington, D.C.

The first African-American owner of this aged brick home was a freed woman called Abigail Sides who bought it in 1849. A succession of other African-Americans owned or rented it before the church bought it in 1920 for use as a community center. This was also the capital's first library for African-Americans.

Continue to the corner house.

2900 O STREET

35 From former South Carolina slave to real estate developer in Georgetown. That's the story of Alfred Pope who resided here before his death in 1906. His granddaughter said he began making big money by employing men to clean the outhouses at night.

Pope owned the land on which Mt. Zion Church stands today, just around the corner, and he built a row of houses from the church to this corner stand. Alfred Pope, one of the earliest African-American entrepreneurs, also owned 10 single family homes and tenements north of Reservoir Road, and a wood and coal yard on 29th Street.

Turn right into 29th St., continuing to the church on the right.

1334 29TH STREET

36 This is the location of the oldest African American congregation in the District of Columbia, tracing its roots back to 1814 when 125 blacks split from Montgomery Street Church because they where segregated by color.

In 1816 they built a church known as The Meeting House at 27th & P Streets. The swelling congregation raised this church in the 1870s on land bought from the noted black real estate developer, Alfred Pope. Many of the congregants, widely dispersed in Washington, D.C., are descendants of the original families, who then lived among a sizeable community of African-Americans in Georgetown. The black population in Georgetown dwindled in the 20th century as real estate values soared.

Continue down 29th St. to the corner. Look diagonally across Dumbarton Ave. to the SE corner.

2820 & 2822 DUMBARTON AVENUE

37 This was the home and office of Drew Pearson, whose nationally- syndicated column, *Washington Merry-Go-Round,* was a staple for millions of newspaper readers until his death in 1969.

Richard Nixon saved Drew Pearson from a savage beating on the columnist's 53rd birthday. Pearson was at the coat-check room of Washington's exclusive Sulgrave Club on Dupont Circle when Senator Joe McCarthy kicked him in the groin and punched him. The flare-up climaxed a running feud between the Wisconsin Republican, then at the height of his campaign of smearing innocents with the Communist tag, and the celebrity newsman who sought to expose him. Nixon, then a U.S. Senator from California, stepped in and pulled the two apart. Later, Nixon said if he hadn't stepped in to pull off McCarthy, the enraged senator "might have killed Pearson."

In 1975 the newsman's widow, Luvie Pearson, sold this house to her son, Tyler Abell, who was Lyndon Johnson's last Chief of Protocol. Tyler's wife, Bess Abell, was Lady Bird Johnson's social secretary.

Turn right into Dumbarton Ave. & left into 30th St. to the long brick building on the left.

1305-1315 30TH STREET

38 The formidable Miss Lydia English operated her fine finishing school for young women of upper crust families in this handsome building for almost four decades leading up to the Civil War. She wrote in her brochure that she would provide her girls with "that amount of mental and moral culture necessary to render them amiable, intelligent and useful members of society."

About 140 girls boarded each year at Miss Lydia English's Georgetown Female Seminary. One of the most famous was Harriet Williams, the teenage bride of the middle-aged Russian minister, whose marital home is located near the end of this walk.

The 1820 building was commandeered for a military hospital immediately after the Union defeat at the First Battle of Bull Run in 1861. Lydia English relocated her school to a smaller building at 2812 N St., where the widow Susan Decatur lived after the death by duel of her husband Stephen in 1820.

Later, the building was converted into apartments, and is now known collectively as The Colonial.

John Mitchell, the only attorney general to serve time in prison, lived in this house.

Continue down to the NW corner building which faces The Colonial.

1300 30TH STREET

39 During the Civil War this was the home of Dr. & Mrs. Grafton Tyler, such ardent Southern sympathizers that they closed their shutters to block the sight of Union troops and their Stars and Stripes at the military hospital across the street. On the eve of the scheduled hanging of her nephew, a spy and saboteur, Mrs. Tyler passed him a message as she kissed him goodbye, then ensured his escape by bribing a guard.

This was also the final home of John Mitchell, the only Attorney General who served time in prison. He was sentenced to 19 months for conspiracy in the Watergate scandal. Mitchell, then estranged from his wife Martha, said after sentencing, "It could have been a hell of a lot worse. They could have sentenced me to spend the rest of my life with Martha Mitchell."

In 1988 he collapsed on the sidewalk half a block from here and died before the ambulance arrived at George Washington University hospital.

Turn right into N St. to the portico of the long mansion on the left.

3014 N STREET

40 This old home, with an original center portion dating back to 1790, was built for the rich tobacco merchant John Laird and inherited by his daughter, Barbara, wife of local judge James Dunlop. President Lincoln blocked Dunlop's advancement because of his Southern sympathies.

The Dunlop family owned the mansion until it was bought in 1912 by Abraham Lincoln's only surviving son, Robert Todd Lincoln, who lived here until his death in 1926.

Robert Todd Lincoln was treated like royalty because he was the son of the legendary 16th president. Being chairman of the Pullman railroad company he was nicknamed "The Prince of Rails." The son did not look at all like the father. Abraham Lincoln was 6' 4" whereas Robert Todd was only 5' 9 1/2". His schoolmates called him "Cockeye" because he was squint in one eye.

In 1875 a tearful Robert Todd Lincoln had a court declare his mother insane and incapable of managing her affairs because she carried stocks and bonds in her clothing, spent money wildly and hallucinated. The following year she was declared "restored to reason" and freed. She despised him for what he had done and it pained him for the rest of his life. The Lincoln line died out with his grandchildren because none of them had children of their own.

In 1983 the mansion was bought by Ben Bradlee, then executive editor of the *Washington Post* and an icon of journalism for steering the paper through the Watergate scandal.

Turn around and look at the house at the top of the multiple steps.

3017 N STREET

41 An unending stream of oglers forced Jackie Kennedy to flee this home just 10 months after she left the White House. She could no longer bear the hordes of people stepping out of cars and chartered buses to catch a glimpse of her. Some people even slept in their cars to have the house under constant watch. Others ate on collapsible card tables taken out of the trunks of their autos. In September 1964 she fled to the peace and quiet of Manhattan.

Jackie had bought it from James Gibson, whose dying wish was to be buried beneath two 37 inch high, blue-gray champagne bottles chiseled from granite. He said his friends should party and not mourn for him. Gibson got his wish until so many sightseers trampled over the grass that officials got rid of the strange memorial.

The 14-room house was built with 12 inch thick walls about 1794, when the magnolia trees were planted.

Secretary of War Newton Baker lived here during World War 1. A former Miss America, Yolande Betbeze Fox, bought it in 1975.

Continue along N St. looking to the left.

3038 N STREET

42 The Secret Service closed this entire block to traffic on a December night in 1992 when President-elect Clinton was guest of honor at a glittering dinner hosted by the widow Pamela Harriman. A top Democratic Party political hostess and fundraiser, she was rewarded with appointment as Ambassador to France.

She inherited this early 19th century house and a multimillion dollar fortune from her third husband, Averell Harriman. Almost 30 years her senior, he was the son of a railroad robber baron though he became more famous in his own right as Ambassador to Moscow, Governor of New York and elder statesman.

Pamela and Averell had been wartime lovers in London when she was newly-married to Prime Minister Winston Churchill's son, Randolph, and he was supervising the Lend-Lease program. In 1971, when they were both recently widowed, they met again at a Georgetown dinner party and married within months. Only then did the English-born Pamela, daughter of Lord Digby, become an American citizen.

After President Kennedy's assassination, Harriman and his first wife, Marie, moved out of this house to allow their friend Jackie Kennedy to move in with her children. Jackie stayed a month before buying the house across the road.

Continue along N St., crossing 31st St., Wisconsin Ave. & Potomac St. to stand on the NW corner of N & Potomac Sts.

3255 N STREET

43 For a while in 1983 it seemed like the entire country was glued to TV watching

Novelist Herman Wouk lived here while writing The Winds of War & War & Remembrance.

the ABC mini-series based on Herman Wouk's novel, *The Winds of War.* The bestselling author, who started out as a gag writer, lived here for decades with his wife and agent, Betty, while writing *Youngblood Hawke* and *War & Remembrance.* He had already won international acclaim for *The Caine Mutiny* and *Marjorie Morningstar.*

Herman and Betty Wouk donated all earnings from a much earlier book, *This Is My God,* to a charitable fund set up by them after their first child drowned in a pool accident in Mexico in

1951. A pious man, Wouk regularly attended the 28th Street synagogue in Georgetown.

Wouk's house and the adjacent three Federal homes were built about 1815 by Walter and Clement Smith and are known as Smith's Row.

Look diagonally across N St., to the 2nd house from the corner of Potomac St.

3260 N STREET

44 John F. Kennedy planted a magnolia tree in the back garden when he lived here from 1951 until his election to the U.S. Senate the following year. A later occupant in the 1960s was Senate Republican leader Hugh Scott of Pennsylvania. He said whenever he met Kennedy, the President would ask "How's my tree?"

Scott was a connoisseur of ancient Chinese and Japanese art and had a huge private collection of oriental ceramics, jade, bronze and other artifacts. He first became interested while learning Japanese grammar when commuting by rail to his Philadelphia law office, then shifted to the older, more sophisticated Chinese art.

New York Times columnist Maureen Dowd bought this house in 1995.

Continue along N St., cross 33rd St. to the 2nd house on the right.

3307 N STREET

45 John F. Kennedy moved into this house in 1957, just three weeks after the birth of his daughter, Caroline, and stayed here until the day he entered the White House.
On the President-elect's last day in this house he rehearsed his inaugural speech in the downstairs library, which he often used as a breakfast room.

John F. Kennedy lived here from 1957 until the morning of his inauguration.

After a Thanksgiving dinner here in 1960, the president-elect flew to his parent's home in Palm Beach, Florida to decide on his new cabinet. Pregnant Jackie stayed behind, not expecting to give birth until a few weeks later but two hours after JFK's plane left National Airport, she was rushed by ambulance from here to Georgetown University hospital. The president-elect had no sooner landed in Florida than he took the faster press plane back to Washington, learning en route that Jackie had already given birth to their son, John.

In 1952, when Bobby Kennedy and his family were living here, his sister, Jean, missed a flight to New York and drove here for dinner. She parked in the street and left her luggage in the car. A thief made off with a suitcase containing jewelry worth $33,000. Police later recovered all of it except a pair of earrings valued at $10,000.

During the Civil War this house was rented out for $250 a month and used as the rectory for nearby St. John's Episcopal Church.

Look diagonally across the road to the left, at the house just off the SW corner of N & 33rd Sts.

3302 N STREET

46 A kindly woman and her elderly father took such pity on newsmen standing in the cold outside President-elect Kennedy's home across the street that the journalists placed a plaque of appreciation on the eastern wall. John F. Kennedy himself presented it to her on Inauguration Day 1961. It commemorates the good deeds of Miss Helen Montgomery and her father, Charles Montgomery, in providing food, warmth and use of the telephone to newsmen. The charitable acts began when a UPI reporter asked if he could use her phone. Helen Montgomery began an open-door policy for the press, providing food and coffee. She died in 1975.

A tablet on the wall also notes this was the last home of Dr. Stephen Bloomer Balch, a Revolutionary War officer and pastor of Georgetown's Bridge Street Presbyterian Church for more than 50 years. When he was in his eighties he moved into this house with his new wife, Jane Parrott. After fire broke out in 1831 he said, "I lost everything but my Parrott." The five houses were saved and subsequently known as Burnt Row.

Return to 33rd St., turn left, stopping at the 1st house on the left.

1310 33RD STREET

47 This house will always be associated with President Reagan's Commerce Secretary Malcolm Baldrige, a Cowboy Hall of Famer who was killed in a calf-roping accident in 1987.

Baldrige, a former rodeo champion, died while practising calf-roping on a California ranch. He had roped the heels of a calf and just released the rope when his horse stumbled and fell on him. On the day of the funeral a traditional cowboy tribute was paid when the same horse was led riderless around the rodeo ring where Baldrige had hoped to perform.

Continue up 33rd St., turn left into O St., looking to the left.

3322 O STREET

48 In the mid-19th century this was the love nest of a middle-aged Russian nobleman and his local teenage wife, known affectionately as *Beauty and The Beast.*

Baron Alexander de Bodisco arrived here in 1838 to head his country's diplomatic legation. He met Harriet Williams at a Christmas party and married her in Georgetown 16 months later when he was 53 and she was just 16. The bride was given away by Henry Clay and VIP guests included President Martin Van Buren and Daniel Webster. They had a happy marriage, six children and entertained lavishly.

On state occasions, Baron de Bodisco was a shimmering presence as locals watched him pass by in a gilded coach with driver and footman resplendent in bright uniforms. When he died in 1854 he was buried in Oak Hill Cemetery beneath an obelisk reminding all that he was "Chamberlain and private counsellor of His Majesty The Emperor of all Russias, his Envoy Extraordinary and Minister Plenipotentiary to the United States." His young widow later married the British military attache and is buried in Portsmouth, England.

This was also the home of Robert E. Lee's mother while he was at West Point. In the 1920s the dilapidated building housed ten apartments until bought and restored by a State Department lawyer.

Sen. John Heinz (R-Pa.) bought it for almost $450,000 after his election to Congress in the early 1970s. His widow, Teresa, lived here with her new husband, Sen. John Kerry (D-Mass).

Look directly across the road.

3327 O STREET

49 A green-eyed, curly-blonde American, hailed by British intelligence as World War 11's "greatest unsung heroine," seduced enemy prey in this house to get them to part with secret codes and ciphers that changed the course of the war. Her real name was Elizabeth Pack but British intelligence gave her the code name *Cynthia.*

Locked in a loveless marriage to a British diplomat 19 years older, the American-born Cynthia made love to others in the line of duty. Just before her death she declared, "I was not a loose woman. I was a patriot."

Cynthia was recruited by allied intelligence in pre-war Poland when the 26-year-old siren tapped into the classified work of the country's pro-Nazi foreign minister by bedding his trusted aides.

Impressed by her performance, the British Secret Service set her up in this discreet little house with instructions to steal the naval ciphers from the

Vichy French embassy in Washington. Years later Cynthia confessed to seducing the French press attache in this house immediately after their first lunch at the Carlton hotel.

Once hooked, he helped her plot an elaborate scheme to copy the ciphers. They deceived the night watchman, telling him they were lovers and needed to meet at the embassy for nightly liaisons away from their spouses. Once he'd grown accustomed to their nightly presence they sneaked in an expert locksmith provided by British intelligence. Known as The Georgia Cracker, he broke open the naval attache's safe and the ciphers were smuggled out, photocopied and returned by 4 am the same night. Cynthia's reward came several months later when American and British troops landed in North Africa with minimal resistance. Only then did she learn how invaluable her charms had been to the allied landings.

After Italy entered the war, Cynthia was told to get hold of the secret Italian naval codes. This time she targeted the naval attache, Admiral Alberto Lais, who had first fallen for her when he was a junior diplomat and she was a mere 14 years old. He had called her his "Golden Girl" when he met her clandestinely for tea and small talk.

Cynthia bewitched him again when she telephoned in 1940 to say "Here's your Golden Girl!" The helpless Italian was reeled into this Georgetown lair where he tipped her off to imminent sabotage of Italian merchant ships blockaded by the British in American harbors. She alerted U.S. naval intelligence, but it was too late. His time-bombs wrecked 25 ships.

Shortly before his deportation, the admiral gave Cynthia the name of another Italian diplomat who cooperated so fully that the secret ciphers were photographed and handed back without any glitches. This time her dangerous wooing helped the British navy cripple Italy's fleet.

After the war Cynthia married the French press attache she had seduced and they lived in their French castle near the Spanish border until her death from cancer in 1963.

Continue to the corner of O & 34th Sts. Look at the large house directly across on the SW corner.

3400 O STREET

50 When Congressman George Bush ran for a U. S. Senate seat from Texas in 1970 he was defeated by Lloyd Bentsen, who came to live here after his victory.

This spacious house was built during the War of 1812 for a man whose job was gauging casks. In the 1920s and 1930s there were commercial businesses on street level, with the entrance to the house on 34th Street. A tailor and dry cleaning business were followed by a grocery store and then a doctor's office.

Bentsen was the Democratic party's nominee for vice president in the 1988 election and later became Treasury Secretary in President Clinton's first term.

Continue down the left side of 34th St. to about mid-way down the block. Look across the road.

1318 34TH STREET

51 When Madeleine Albright and her husband Joe divorced in 1982 after 23 years of marriage, she got this townhouse as part of the settlement. They had met at the *Denver News* in 1957 when he was a reporter and heir to a newspaper chain and she had a summer job in the newspaper's morgue. They married three days after she graduated from Wellesley College.

She was born Marie Jana Korbel in Prague and nicknamed Madeleine by a grandmother. The family fled the Nazis in 1938 and then the Communists, who sentenced her diplomat father to death in absentia for political crimes. The family lived in Prague, London and Belgrade before she was 10. In Belgrade she was taught by a governess because her father didn't want her attending schools with Communists. At 10 years old she entered a Swiss boarding school where she learned French. She is probably the most multilingual of all previous Secretaries of State, speaking English, Czech, French, Russian, Polish and having an understanding of Serbian.

The refugee family arrived in America in 1948 and the following year settled in Colorado where her father taught international relations at the University of Denver.

While preparing her doctoral dissertation on the role of the media in the 1968 Czech democracy movement, she had the good fortune to have Zbigniew Brzezinski as her supervisor, before he became Jimmy Carter's National Security Adviser. Along the way to the top she was also chief legislative assistant to Senator Edmund Muskie and a professor of international affairs at Georgetown University.

In the early years of the Republic Abigail Adams was gently scoffed at by her husband for suggesting women's rights. With her appointment as Secretary of State in 1997 Madeleine Albright held the most senior portfolio in the President's cabinet.

For an optional detour continue down to the corner, turn right into N St. & left into 35th, looking to the block-long college dorm on the right.

If you do not take the detour, turn left into N St., picking up the narrative at stop #56.

WEST SIDE OF 1200 BLOCK, 35TH ST.

52 President Bill Clinton stayed in room 225 of this college dorm, Loyola Hall, after arriving for his freshman year at Georgetown University in the fall of 1964. It was the only college he applied to while a high school senior in Hot Springs, Arkansas.

He quickly distinguished himself as a leader among the 4195 undergraduates with election as president of the freshman class. Later he would also be elected sophomore class president and chairman of the Student Athletics Commission, and win a prestigious Rhodes Scholarship to Oxford University in England. Clinton was enrolled in the School of Foreign Service at Georgetown University and graduated in 1968.

Continue along 35th St., turn right into Prospect St. until opposite the house at the end of the walled garden.

3508 PROSPECT STREET

53 One of the oldest homes in Georgetown, this is believed to have been built between 1788 and 1793 when occupied by Gen. James Maccubbin Lingan, a Revolutionary War hero, prosperous businessman, local civic leader and victim of a murderous mob.

Lingan, 61, was tortured to death in 1812 after going to pro-war Baltimore with Georgetown publisher Alexander Hanson to support a free press and denounce the war with Britain. The mob dragged him out of protective custody in jail, then beat and kicked him to death. His remains were re-interred in Arlington National Cemetery in 1908.

From 1947-1949 this was the home of the first

A Baltimore mob tortured to death the Revolutionary War hero who lived here.

Secretary of Defense, James Forrestal, who jumped to his death from the 16th floor of the Bethesda Naval Hospital seven weeks after resigning from office in 1949.

After his death it became a residence for VIP visitors from abroad when President Truman moved to Blair House, until then the official government guest house on Pennsylvania Avenue, while workmen gutted and reinforced the structural interior of the White House. Among world leaders who stayed here were the Shah of Iran, French President Vincent Auriol and Field Marshall Viscount Montgomery of Alamein.

Return to 35th St. looking across the road to the NE corner brick mansion.

3425 PROSPECT STREET

54 This old house, built in 1798 with 15 inch partitions between the rooms, was the home of maverick physician Dr. Charles Worthington during the War of 1812. He was so against the war with England that he rejoiced when they burned Washington in 1814. After the battle of Bladensburg he treated wounded British soldiers here and accepted from one of them a gold snuff box in gratitude for his "extreme kindness and attention." Worthington refused to follow fashion, wearing his hair in a pony tail and dressing with knee-breeches, long stockings and buckles on his shoes long after they went out of style.

The house was also home to Augustin de Iturbide, grandson of an Emperor of Mexico. After he was exiled from Mexico for criticizing the Republican government, Augustin taught Spanish and French at his alma mater, Georgetown University. He lived here after his marriage in 1915 to Mary Louise Kearney, who had been born in this house.

Sir Willmott Lewis died in this home in 1950 after almost three decades in Washington as correspondent of the venerable London *Times.* Asked what difference it would make after he was knighted by the British monarch in 1931, Sir Willmott replied, "I'll tell you, my boy. Willmott Lewis used to fetch $250 a lecture. Sir Willmott Lewis gets $500!" His widow sold the house to the patrician Rhode Island Democrat, Claiborne Pell, who served six terms in the U.S. Senate and chaired the Foreign Relations Committee.

Continue down Prospect St., looking at the stone mansion on the right, at the SW corner of 34th St.

3400 PROSPECT STREET

55 The original core of this mansion, Halcyon House, was built by the first Secretary of the Navy, Benjamin Stoddert, in 1786. In about 1900 the new owner, Albert Clemens, an eccentric nephew of Mark Twain, made so many additions that critics savaged the maze as "an architectural nightmare."

It decayed and rotted until the 1980s when sculptor John Dreyfuss and his portrait photographer wife, Mary Noble Ours, began years of restoration. Halcyon House has one of the best views overlooking Key Bridge and Roosevelt Island, with lawns swooping down over a number of terraces beautified with rectangular pools and polished metal sculptures by Dreyfuss. His large subterranean studio was hacked deep below the terraces.

Turn left into 34th St. and right into N St., looking to your left.

3327-3339 N STREET

56 These red brick townhouses have been known as Cox's Row ever since Col. John Cox, a former Mayor of Georgetown (1823-45) built them about 1817.

It is said that the civic leader, Mayor Cox, filled the vacant No. 3337 with furniture for a reception for the Marquis de Lafayette in 1824, when the idolized Frenchman returned triumphantly for the first time since helping out in the Revolutionary War.

Walk a few paces down to the house adjacent to Cox's Row.

3325 N STREET

57 Shortly after noon on Monday, October 12, 1964, Georgetown artist Mary Pinchot Meyer was walking alone along the C & O Canal towpath 3/4 of a mile west of Key Bridge, where she had often strolled with her friend Jackie Kennedy in pre-White House days. Suddenly a man accosted her. She screamed and struggled but he shot her once in the chest and again in the left temple. The 43-year-old abstract painter died instantly.

She left behind a sensational handwritten diary in her studio at this address. Years would pass before the public learned that Mary Pinchot Meyer's diary left no doubt she was President Kennedy's lover while he occupied the White House. At the time of the affair she was divorced from Cord Meyer, a former CIA covert agent.

The day after the murder James Angleton, chief of counter-intelligence at the CIA, was discovered searching her Georgetown house at 1523 34th Street. Later that day he was caught trying to pick the lock of her studio here. Angleton and his wife Cicely were close friends of the victim but he left empty-handed.

The diary was found by the victim's sister, Tony Bradlee, and her husband, Ben Bradlee, then Washington bureau chief for *Newsweek.* Years later Ben Bradlee wrote that Kennedy was clearly her lover though he was not identified by name.

In a curious turn, the Bradlees gave the diary to Angleton to get rid of. Years later Tony Bradlee reclaimed it after learning it was still in existence. Then she destroyed it herself. More than a decade after the murder Angleton theorized there might have been a Soviet spy so high in the U.S. government that perhaps JFK and Meyer knew him, and that she may have been murdered because she could expose him.

Mary Meyer's murder was never solved. A 26-year-old laborer from Southeast Washington was arrested within an hour of the murder, walking close by near the Potomac river. His clothes were soaked and his right hand bloodied. He told police he had fallen asleep while fishing and cut his hand trying to grip a rock as he slid down. He was charged with murder but acquitted at the trial.

Continue to the adjacent house on the same side of the street.

3321 N STREET

58 Former *Washington Post* executive editor Ben Bradlee credited the beginnings of his close friendship with John F. Kennedy to his luck in buying this house shortly before Kennedy purchased his a few doors down in 1957. They first met wheeling their newborn in baby carriages.

Bradlee wrote that Kennedy knew he was taking notes of their private conversations, and agreed Bradlee could use any of it so long as he waited until Kennedy had been out of the White House at least five years. After Kennedy's assassination, Bradlee used the material for his book, *Conversations with Kennedy.* Jackie Kennedy disapproved of the book's profanity and icily ended their friendship.

Continue on N St., cross 33rd and Potomac Sts. to Wisconsin Ave., at the commercial heart of Georgetown.

The capital's oldest building is a carpenter's shop and home at 3051 M St., Georgetown.

INDEX

Abell, Tyler & Bess 36
Acheson, Dean & Alice 4, 20, 23
Adams, Abigail & John 49
Adams, John Quincy 2, 7
Agger, Carolyn 7
Albright, Madeleine 48
Alcott, Louisa May 3
Angleton, James 54
Balch, Stephen 44
Baldrige, Malcolm 45
Beall, Ninian 1
Belin, Lamot 17
Bell, Alexander Graham 4
Bentsen, Lloyd 48
Biddle, Francis 9
Bliss, Robert & Mildred 7
Bodisco, Alexander de 45
Bowles, Chester 16
Bradlee, Ben 39, 54, 55
Bradlee, Tony 54
Brown, J. Carter 32
Bush, George 48
Calhoun, John C. 7
Chambers, Whittaker 22
Chesapeake & Ohio Canal 2
Christ Episcopal Church 30
Civil War 2, 3, 36
Clinton, Bill 1, 31, 40, 48, 50
Colonial Dames of America 19
Cooke, Henry 14, 15
Corcoran, William Wilson 16
Cox, John 53
Davidson, Samuel 17
Daw, Reuben 21
de Iturbide, Augustin 52
Dickens, Charles 2
Dodd, Thomas 28
Dodge, Francis 14, 16
Dodge, Robert 16
Dowd, Maureen 42
Downing, Andrew Jackson 15
Dreyfuss, John 53
Dulles, Allen 18, 28
Dulles, Eleanor 28
Dulles, John Foster 31
Dumbarton House 18, 19
Dumbarton Oaks 7
Dunlop, James & Barbara 38
English, Lydia 36
Eustis, Edith 16
Evermay 17
Forrestal, James 51
Fortas, Abe 7
Frankfurter, Felix 6, 23, 32
Georgetown library 5
Georgetown University 1, 2, 24, 38, 43, 49, 50
Grant, Lewis 17
Grant, Ulysess S. & Julia 6, 14
Gray, Boyden 17
Greely, Adolphus 29
Halcyon House 53
Halleck, Henry 6
Hanson, Alexander 2, 50
Harriman, Averell 40
Harriman, Marie 40

Harriman, Pamela 40
Healy, Patrick 1
Heinz, John 46
Heritage House 34
Herter, Christian 28
Hiss, Alger 22
Ickes, Harold 31
Ihlder, John 22
Johnson, Lyndon 7, 18, 36
Joyce, John 6
Kelley, Kitty 32
Kennedy, Bobby 16, 21, 44
Kennedy, Eunice 12
Kennedy, Jackie 21, 32, 39, 43, 54, 55
Kennedy, Jean 44
Kennedy, Joe & Rose 25
Kennedy, John F. 12, 18, 21, 25, 42, 43, 44, 54, 55
Kerrey, John & Teresa 46
Key, Francis Scott 2, 24, 30
Kissinger, Henry 24, 25, 32
Krushchev, Nina 28
Laird, John 38
Lance, Bert & LaBelle 31
Lewis, Sinclair 12
Lewis, Willmott 52
Libbey, John 25
Lincoln, Abraham 37
Lincoln, Mary Todd 38
Lincoln, Robert Todd 38
Lingan, James Maccubbin 50
Linthicum, Edward 23
Madison, Dolley 2, 18
McCarthy, Joe 9, 35, 36
McLean, Evalyn Walsh, 5
Meyer, Mary Pinchott, 54
Mitchell, John, 37
Montgomery, Charles & Helen, 44
Mt. Zion Church 34, 35
Nixon, Richard 22, 35, 36
Oak Hill Cemetery 4, 21, 45
Old Stone House 1, 56
Pack, Elizabeth 46
Payne, John Howard 4
Pearson, Drew 35
Pell, Claiborne 52
Peter, Britannia 10, 31
Peter, Martha Custis 10
Pope, Alfred 34
Porter, Katherine Anne 11
Reed, Walter 14
Roosevelt, Franklin 6
Scott, Hugh 42
Stanton, Edwin 4
Taft, Robert 8, 9
Thomas, Dylan 9
Thomas, George 25
Thornton, William 10
Truman, Harry 21
Tudor Place 10
Tyler, Grafton 37
Vance, Cyrus 32
Volta Bureau 4
Williams, Harriet 36, 45
Woodward, Bob 13
Worthington, Charles 52
Wouk, Herman 41
Zeller, Mary 23